ATTENTION'S LOOP

A Sculptor's Reverie on the Coexistence of Substance and Spirit

ELIZABETH KING

Photographs by Katherine Wetzel

HARRY N. ABRAMS, INC., PUBLISHERS

For my father and for Carlton

The second nen, which illuminates and reflects upon the immediately preceding
nen, also does not know anything about itself. What will become aware of it
is another reflecting action of consciousness that immediately follows in turn.
This action is a further step in self-consciousness. It consolidates the earlier levels.
We shall call it the third nen. This third nen will think, for example, "I know I
noticed I had been thinking, 'It's fine today.'" Or it may say, "I know I was aware
of my knowing that I noticed I had been thinking, 'It's fine today.'"
(Katsuki Sekida, *Zen Training, Methods and Philosophy*)

And all the paradoxes of science and of literature arise from our attempt to
speak simultaneously of ourselves both as knowing selves and as known objects.
(Jacob Bronowski, *The Origins of Knowledge and Imagination*)

CONTENTS

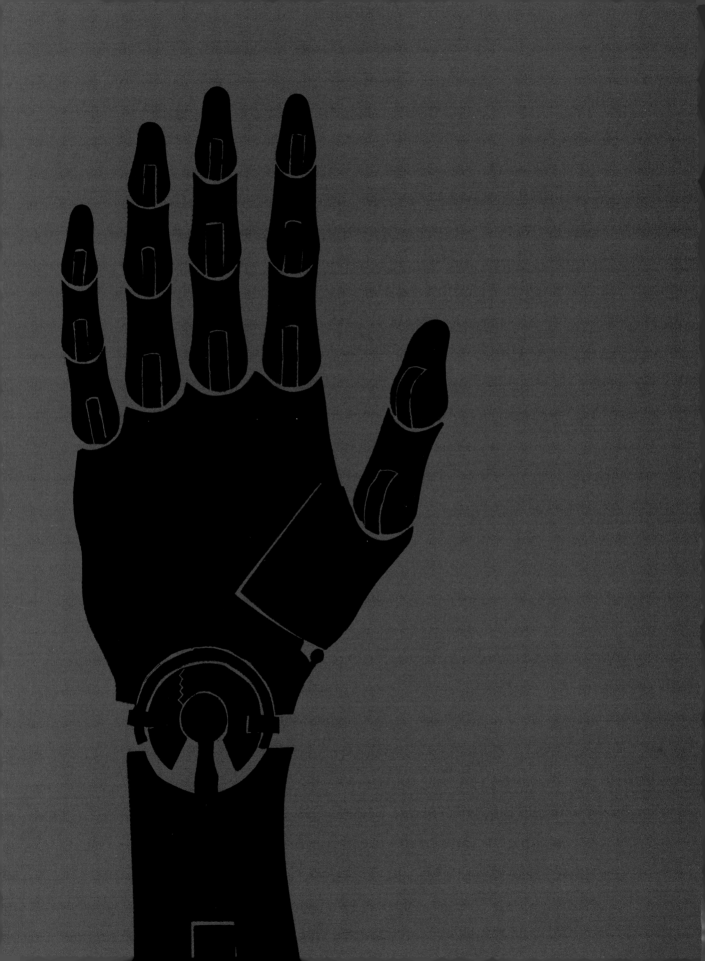

FOREWORD

This is a book about attention and memory. I am a sculptor, so it is also a book about size, dirt, artifice, work, and eye. The text is a set of stories and interruptions that pile up to make a play of overlapping loops. My organizing principle is the image of the round-trip, so one may open the book and step into it at any point. Most of Katherine Wetzel's photographs are of a single sculpture. It is a self-portrait, a particular kind of round-trip, and it is small: one-half life-size. Called *Pupil*, it is jointed and movable, and I pose it. I think of it as an instrument.

I ask my teacher in school, "Mr. Geis, what is a homunculus?"
"The little man in your eye," Bill Geis tells me. Years
go by. One day, the phrase "Tom Thumb in the horse's ear"
occurs to me, and I realize I've been mindlessly repeating
it for months. I know where it's from: Gaston Bachelard
on the subject of miniature. Here it is, in *The Poetics of Space*,
Bachelard's Petit Poucet. "He is an ear within an ear,"
says Bachelard. "A Cartesian philosopher – if a Cartesian
could indulge in pleasantry – would say that, in this story,
Petit Poucet is the pineal gland of the plough."[1]

What again is the story of Tom Thumb? One version
appears in the *Household Tales* of the Brothers Grimm.

There was once a poor farmer who was sitting by the hearth one evening and poking the fire, while his wife was spinning nearby.

"How sad that we have no children!" he said. "It's so quiet here, and other homes are full of noise and life."

"Yes," his wife responded with a sigh. "If only we had a child, just one, even if it were tiny and no bigger than my thumb, I'd be quite satisfied. We'd surely love him with all our hearts."

Now it happened that the wife fell sick, and after seven months she gave birth to a child that was indeed perfect in every way but no bigger than a thumb.

"It's just as we wished," they said, "and he shall be dear to our hearts."

Because of his size they named him Thumbling. Although they fed him a great deal, the child did not grow any bigger but stayed exactly as he was at birth. Still, he had an intelligent look and soon revealed himself to be a clever and nimble fellow who succeeded in all his endeavors.

One day the farmer was getting ready to chop wood in the forest, and he said to himself, "If only there were someone who could drive the wagon into the forest after me."

"Oh, Father," cried Thumbling, "I'll take care of the wagon. You can count on me. It'll be in the forest whenever you want it."

The man laughed and said, "How're you going to manage that? You're much too small to handle the reins."

"That's not important," Thumbling said. "I just need Mother to hitch the horse, and I'll sit down in his ear and tell him which way to go."

"Well," answered the father. "Let's try it once."

When the time came, the mother hitched up the horse and put Thumbling in his ear. Then the little fellow shouted commands. "Giddyap! Whoa! Giddyap!" Everything went quite well, as if a master were at the reins, and the wagon drove the right way toward the forest. As it took a turn and the little fellow cried out "Giddyap! Giddyap!" two strangers happened to come along.

"My word!" said one of them. "What's that? There goes a wagon without a driver, and yet, I hear a voice calling to the horse."

THUMBLING

"There's something strange going on here," said the other. "Let's follow the wagon and see where it stops."

The wagon drove right into the forest up to the spot where the wood was being chopped. When Thumbling saw his father, he called out to him, "You see, Father, here I am with the wagon! Now just get me down."

The father grabbed the horse with his left hand, and with his right he took his little son out of its ear. Then Thumbling plopped himself sprightly on a piece of straw. When the two men caught sight of him, they were so amazed that they could not open their mouths. One of the men took the other aside and said, "Listen, that little fellow could make our fortune if we exhibit him in the big city for money. Let's buy him."

They went to the farmer and said, "Sell us the little man, and we'll see to it that he's treated well."

"No," answered the farmer, "he's the apple of my eye, and I wouldn't sell him for all the gold in the world."[2]

The apple of my eye! But Thumbling talks his father into selling him for "a tidy sum," whispering in his ear, "I'll manage to get back soon," and rides off on the brim of a stranger's hat. He escapes down a mousehole, falls in with bad company, is eaten accidentally by a cow, and extracts himself from assorted misfortunes, thwarting burglars, butchers, and kidnappers, for "indeed, there is a great deal of sorrow and misery in this world!" At last, through resourceful use of accident, he finds his way back home.

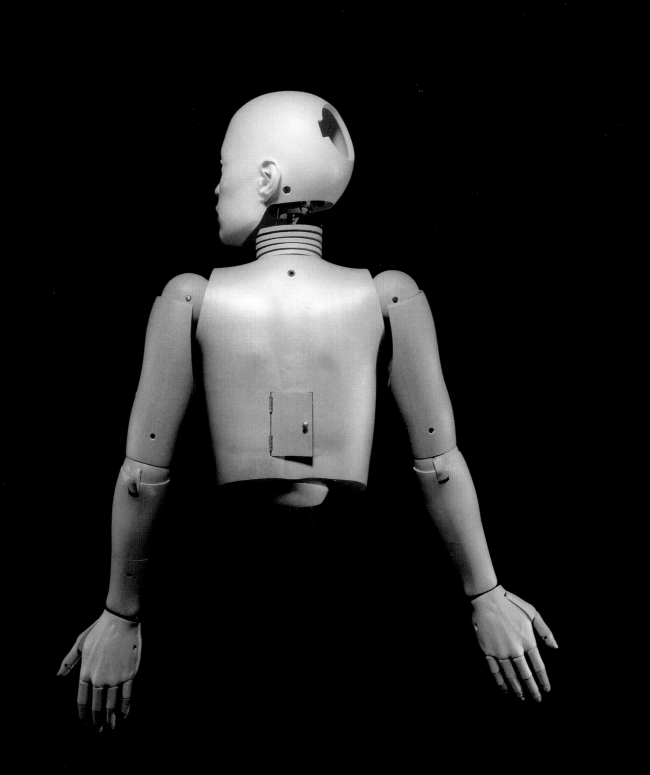

Thumbling, or Tom Thumb, or Hop-'0-my-Thumb – these are some of his English names. He goes all the way back to King Arthur, a tiny swordsman in one century, a farmer, a woodsman, a wanderer in the next. "You little extract of a man!" a thief cries in one translation. He is a student of the relations between ingenuity and smallness. The apple of his father's eye.

Figure 1

We have two "pupils." One, an English word for student, comes from the Latin *pupillus*, little boy or ward or orphan. "The apple of the eye" is among the meanings given for the second "pupil" in the Oxford English Dictionary, which quotes a 1398 text, "The Blacke of theye . . . is callyd Pupilla in latyn for smalle ymages ben seen therin." So the aperture of the eye comes from the word for orphan girl, the Latin feminine form *pupilla*. In Greek too, the word κόρη means little girl, doll, and also pupil of the eye, and was originally a children's expression referring to the miniature reflection of oneself seen by looking closely at another's eye.[3]

The word homunculus, for that matter, has its own complicated ancestry. With a Latin suffix for the diminutive, and an Indo-European root that links it to the words for earth and earthling – one sprung from the land (humus, chthonic, autochthon) – it is connected to the words humble, human, and humane. A helpful miniature being, made of dirt, one might venture. That this speck of dirt gets in our eye, or our ear, this is the germ of the story.

I.

In the twelfth century, Adelard of Bath (fl. 1116–42), an English Scholastic philosopher and traveler, pioneering the beginnings of Western awareness of Arabic thought, declared his theory of visual perception:

… in the brain is generated a certain subtle air, having the same nature as fire, which passes through the optic nerve and exits through the pupil; this "visual spirit" or "fiery virtue" then passes with marvelous swiftness to the visible body, where it is impressed with the form of the body. Returning to its place, the visual spirit communicates this form to the observer's soul.[4]

Adelard is questioned by his nephew about this theory.

First, inquires the nephew, is the visual spirit substance or accident? Corporeal substance, replies Adelard. In that case, insists the nephew, it is madness to suppose that when we open our eyes, the visual spirit can travel to the fixed stars and back in the instant required for the act of vision to be performed … Adelard defends himself by noting, in the first place, that one must not underestimate the "exceedingly swift motion of the visual spirit," which is "more subtly perfected than all things compounded of the elements by the marvelous means of the Creator's power," and second that it is not certain that the fixed stars are quite so far away as some think. The nephew then raises a second objection, perhaps even more serious than the first, noting the possibility of the eyelid being closed while the visual spirit is out on mission. Adelard's response, in addition to a further reminder that the spirit's swiftness must not be underestimated, is that the visual spirit is the soul's agent, and the soul (which controls the opening and closing of the eye) will surely not close the door in such a way as to injure itself or its agent. Third, Adelard's nephew objects that if we behold an object continuously for some time, since our perception of the object is continuous, the visual spirit must simultaneously go and come and must therefore interfere with itself. Adelard again replies, in a now familiar vein, that the visual spirit moves so swiftly that the interval is insensible, and therefore vision seems continuous even though it is not. Finally, the nephew inquires how one is to understand the impressing of forms on the soul when the visual spirit returns to the observer.[5]

And here is the great question: how and where does sensation become perception? We're still arguing about it. Adelard, "assuming an Augustinian stance," explains to his nephew that since the soul is incorporeal, the sensible forms presented to it by the visual spirit induce out of the soul's own abundance a likewise incorporeal form, an intellectual double.[6]

THREE KINDS OF ROUND-TRIP

3.

Tom Thumb himself, apple of his father's eye, is a kind of soul's agent. Quick, corporeal, and tiny, he even passes through other bodies on his way back to home's body. He extends himself into the world, carrying the memory of hearth's fire, and returns to tell what he's seen.[9]

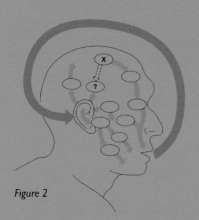

Figure 2

2.

Goes Outside the Body and Comes Back In

I saw this picture recently in a book (Figure 2).

It describes the way speech and hearing make possible a loop that can connect two parts of the mind otherwise inaccessible to one another.[7] What if even the most fleeting ruminative fragment of our mental life involves immediate sensation or body motion – or the memory of them? Then these phenomena, especially as they are articulated and broadcast by works of art, must be central to the unfolding of our conscious relations with the world. Attention goes outside the body and comes back in, to make thought. Not unlike medieval Adelard declared. The sensorium: ear, eye, nose, hand, the moving limbs . . . we give form to thoughts in order to have them.[8]

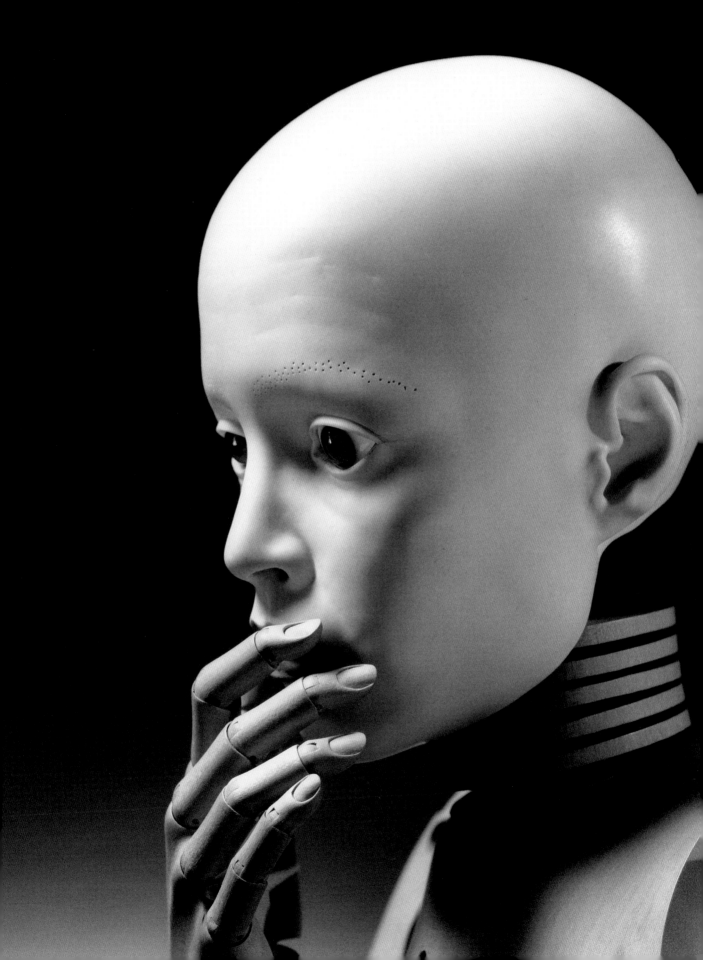

THE SIZES OF THINGS IN THE MIND'S EYE

Photographs seldom deliver things in their actual sizes (the eye in this picture is one-half inch in diameter, the size of a marble). One may be astonished, for example, at the size of a Giacometti sculpture seen first in a photograph. But memory itself changes the size of a thing, and so when you go a second time to see that sculpture, you are hit again, with a different, a more complex, kind of surprise.

[Giacometti] points out that, among sculptures produced by early civilisations and by prehistoric man, there is a fairly common size for a figure and for a head and that this size is relatively small, and he suggests: "I think that this actually was the size that instinctively seemed right, the size one really sees things. And in the course of history, perception has been mentally transposed into concept. I can do your head life-size because I know it's life-size.[10] *I don't see directly anymore, I see you through my knowledge.*[11] In this comment made to David Sylvester, Giacometti pries open the gap between object and object-seen: between object and subject. Either he sees me as I really am, or he sees me as he really sees. But how does he really see? In part, with his hands. His sculpture records the inconstancy of perception. And it records the battle between hand and eye — the organ that touches and the organ that looks — each of which operates in a different zone of proximity. Things constantly changed size in Giacometti's hands. Things got smaller.

Do we judge the sizes of objects, persons, and places, relative to our own body? But we ourselves never quite feel a fixed size. We are large one moment, small the next.

Memory changes the sizes of things. Even the memory of a moment ago. Drawing from life and drawing from memory are the same, Wayne Thiebaud tells us, the first is just a shorter delay.[12] And the eye never sees any but the smallest of things all at once. It flits across the surfaces of the visible like a darter, and the mind is collecting spots of light in an ocean. When I close my eyes and conjure the house where I grew up, it is not a fixed image, but a set of tiny movements, now right, now left, that I perform in time. Close-hand looking loses the thing seen, becomes temporal. To get a good look at something, we back up, we make the thing small. And to remember it?

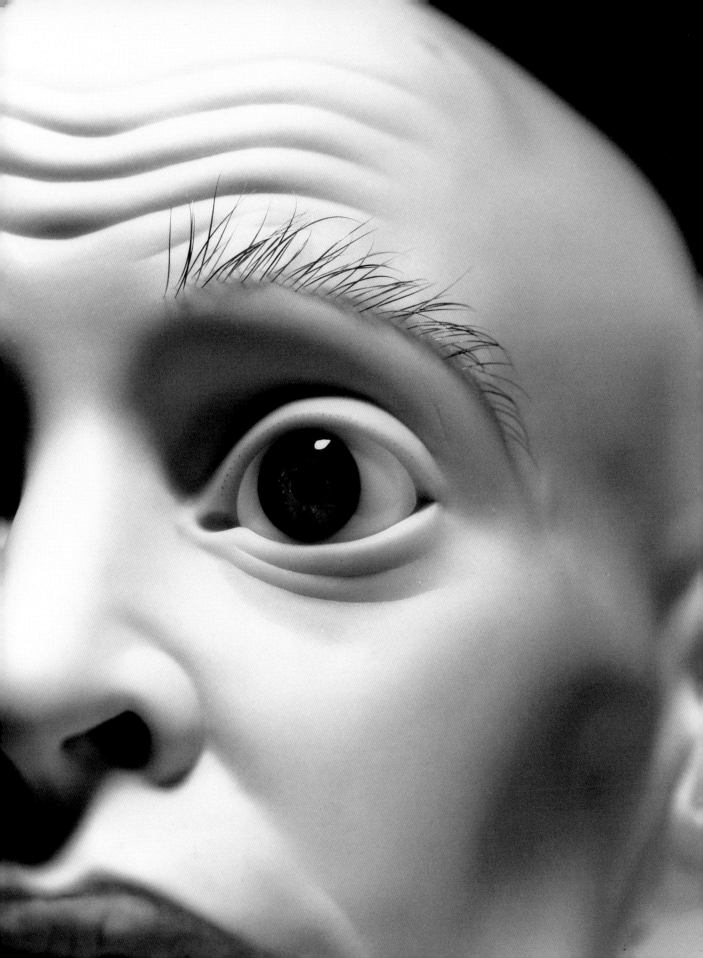

The mind constructs things on its own scale. And our ancient habit is still to conceive our head as our private chamber, a room we furnish and whose occupant is us.

As a child in Michigan I once had a small bean: an amulet made of some kind of hollowed shell, about the size and shape of a navy bean. It had a lid with a tiny knob on it, and when you uncorked it you could shake out onto your palm twelve ivory (ivory!) elephants, each smaller than this letter n. Other children wanted this thing and bargained with me. I would like to have it now, to check on its size. I try and imagine it. Still moving from hand to hand? Or stashed, plowed under, planted? Memory returns again and again to occupy this bean. Out of, into, the bean: something larger than itself.

I am lost in thought, moving about in my mind in a familiar room.

Suddenly, with shock, I realize I am *in* that exact room. A tiny shift of

attention and one room explodes into another. In bursts all the

light, air, and sound of the here and now. What is this shift, in and of

itself? I'd like to be watching at the moment of this interruption in

someone else's reverie, to see what it looks like from the outside.

Maybe the head makes an imperceptible jerk, the eyelids flicker. It

could look like almost nothing! Or take the return trip: the precise

instant when a child ceases paying attention and slips into daydream.

All but invisible: the eyes stop seeing the world in front of them.

But what has really changed on the face? Perhaps only that two pupils

release their convergence on your own face a few feet away, a

movement the width of a hair.

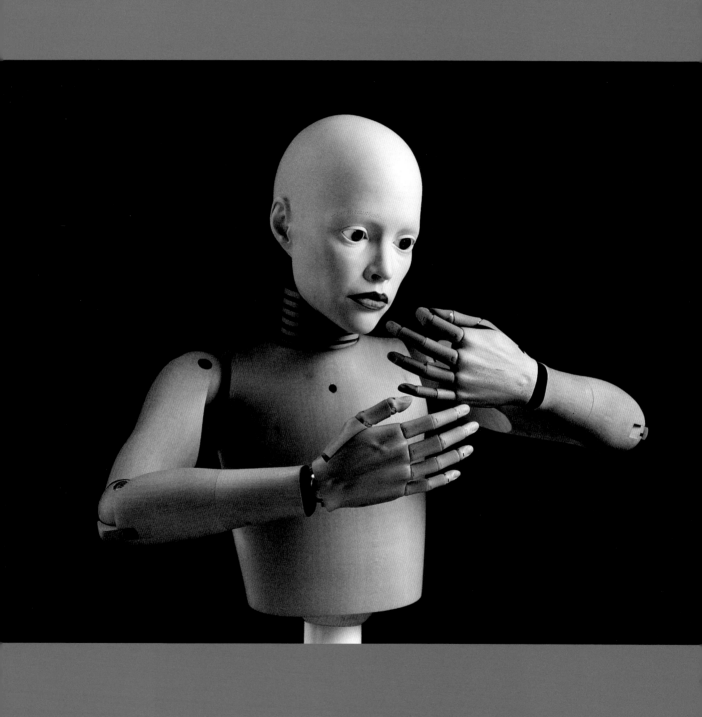

One day my father, a physicist, told me about a copper crystal he had

inherited from a scientist at Oak Ridge. It was grown in the lab to be struc-

turally perfect, having only 3,000 dislocations per cubic centimeter instead

of the normal 10,000,000. If you held it between your thumb and forefinger

and squeezed it even slightly, you'd ruin it. Dad was wondering how he

could slice a thin wafer (only a few molecules thick), off this crystal, so he

could examine it with the neutron beam: "What if I just drape a thread

over it, and put each end of the thread in an acid, so that it will slowly cut

through the copper without exerting any pressure?"

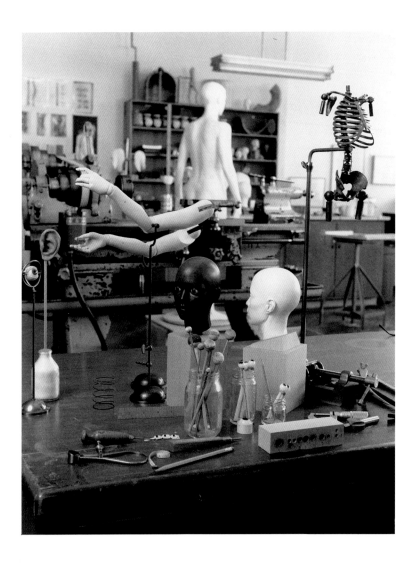

Degree of Difficulty

"Can this be physically done?" is the
question that launches my actions
in the studio. If I invent a good enough
problem, this problem, together with
the laws of nature it will bring me
up against, plus a deadline, will save
me from the poverty of my intent.

For example, I'm trying to do two things at the same time: to make something that looks like a hand – its image – but also to make it behave like a hand, do what a hand does: move, point, grasp, put. In this contest between image and object (ghost and machine) I am eager for the tension that results in the finished work from making one form of representation collide with another.

Both sides sustain damage. The hand moves along sculpturally enough, but abruptly the thumb is sliced off and forced back on again with a ball-and-socket joint. At the same time, a less-than-full rotation at the base of the thumb prevents the hand from disintegrating into a robotic claw. One thing is fixed by breaking part of another.

In an automaton or a puppet, movement is bought at the price of the image. You could say that the image is damaged to permit mechanical motion. How to make a moving mouth presents an interesting problem to a wood carver. Donald Keene, describing the evolution of the Japanese theater of Bunraku, observed that for every step towards realism, there was a concomitant step away from it.[13] A puppet's gestures, as they become more and more sensitive, finally require the actions of three puppeteers, all of whom are fully visible with the puppet on the stage. The contradiction itself fuels our engagement, hypnotizes us.

In one Bunraku character, Gabu, a hidden seam at the jawline can open to represent the movement of the mouth. But then the puppet maker went one step further. The seam goes on opening, and the whole head transforms from a beautiful girl into an ogress.[14]

This puppet was meant to turn into a monster. But an unsummoned monster can appear, unless the artist is careful.

Figure 3a   Figure 3b

Cascade

Work proceeds as a series of self-interruptions. For example, you take a small block of wood to the bandsaw to cut it into a stack of thin layers. But first you have to make a jig to hold the block, so as not to cut your fingers. You make an unnecessarily elegant jig, in private indulgence.

Back at the saw with the jig, you're setting up a fence so all of the slices will be the same thickness, when you think: if I want a hole up through this stack of layers I'd better drill it now while the block is still solid.

You think forward and move backward. The wood wafers are going to be a movable neck, built like a stack of plates over a flexible, brass ball-and-socket "spine" inside. So the hole is for the internal movable parts. Yes, drill the hole before cutting the block into slats.

Should the hole be in the center? Spines are more towards the backs of necks. Suddenly three big problems loom.
1. How does the neck distribute itself about the spine, so I can locate and direct the hole?
2. Should I carve the neck first and then cut it into slices, or slice it first and then clamp the slices temporarily back together to carve it?

3. How big a hole?

You sit down and draw a diagram of the neck. When the head tilts to one side or the other, how much clearance is necessary between the outer wood slats and the joints inside? You make a movable paper model of the individual parts, marveling over the invention of scissors, and then paper itself, stopping to examine a cut edge in the magnifying glass. You've been worrying about these brass joints. For the last neck you made, you used gooseneck from a lamp store and later hated the way the gooseneck rebounded a little out of the exact position you wanted. You would place the head and neck in a given pose, and when you took your hands off it, there would be a tiny return motion, goosenecks being nothing more than restrained springs. This was completely unacceptable.

You think backward and move forward: this time I'm going to make the joints from scratch. It might be possible to achieve all the motions of the

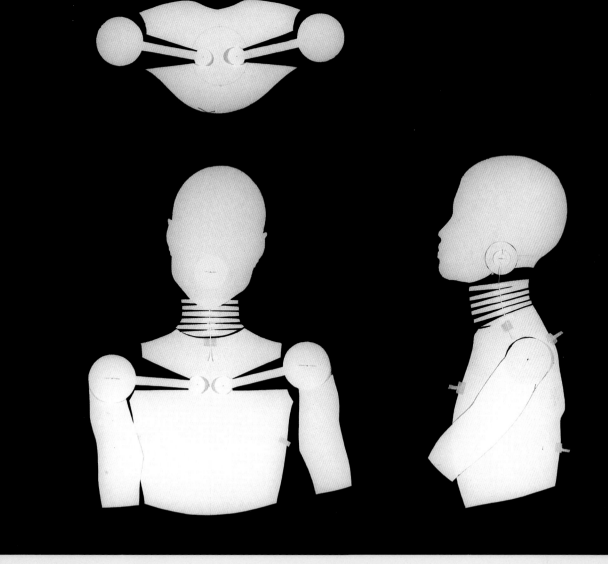

neck and head with two ball-and-socket units, one at the top and one at the bottom of the neck. The rigid shaft between them will be hidden within the neck slats, and these will take up the movement and make it look like the whole length of the neck is flexing.

These joints... they've got to be very small and very strong; they should be spring-loaded and adjustable for the right tension. And not too heavy. You set about designing the parts and move to the lathe.

The block of the wood, the jig, the saw, and the drill wait.

The self-portrait takes the immediate circumstances of *being* as its subject: the self a laboratory, the portrait an inquiry. In the extraordinary Kubelka film *Pause!* (1977)[15] Arnulf Rainer practically tries to climb down his own throat to get inside of himself, to see what is there, and likewise he tries to climb out of himself, to look back from the outside. Is it Narcissus who first discovers he is a self? Perhaps what really fascinated him in that reflection was the momentary *escape* from self: a seeming glimpse from the outside, of the boundary between self and world. He is our first philosopher. His story is our own reflection, and it is present in

the philosopher's definition of consciousness as a property of the mind that can think about its own thinking.

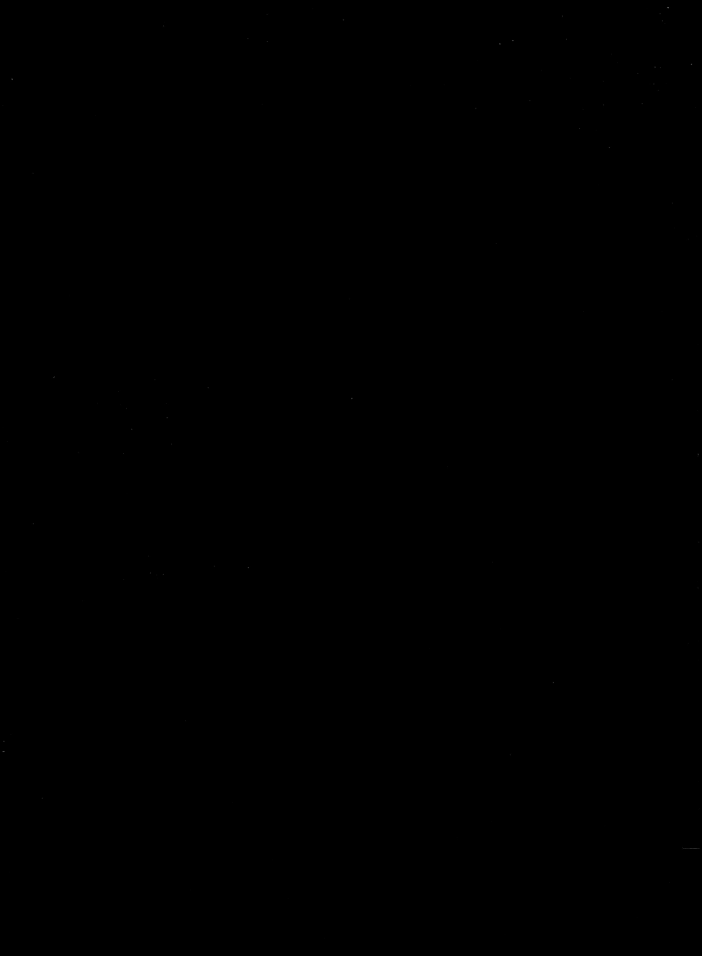

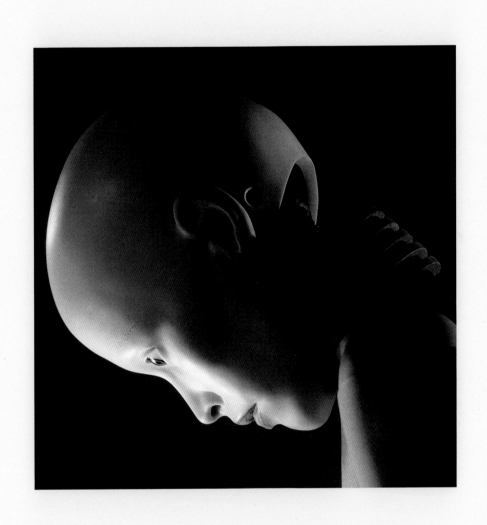

The Corridoio of the Uffizi, near windowless, snaking

through Florence and over the Ponte Vecchio to the

Pitti Palace, is hung for its entire one-half-kilometer

length with artists' self-portraits. Raphael, Rembrandt,

Velázquez, Delacroix . . . face after face directly records

the painter's act of scrutiny. Eye, mirror, hand, paint,

easel, eye. From hand's office to eye's home and back.

We step briefly into each loop, appalled by the glare.

38

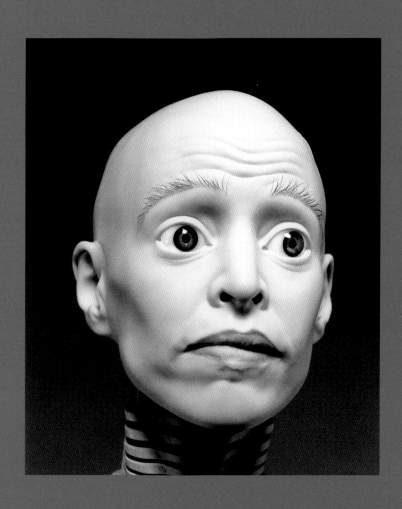

Impossible to freeze
the moment of regard

Figure 4a

Sculptures don't exactly look back at us. We can't ever quite maneuver into the seeming line of sight. In a painting, there is always a setting, even if just the canvas itself, and we experience the sitter's gaze as situated in time and place. But in sculpture, its very "hereness"[16] promises the possibility of direct eye contact. Sculptors have always worried about this. Someone should write a history of art's efforts to depict the eye. ("I want a History of Looking," Roland Barthes wrote in *Camera Lucida*.)

The Egyptian sculptors made eyes of glass, the Greek made them of stone with inlaid silver for the whites, the Roman remained faithful to the eye's blank form alone. Michelangelo carved the eye into a socket of exaggerated depth, carved the iris as a raised island, the pupil a pond, and the sun's reflection over the pupil a little peninsula: the play of light on the stone surface gives the illusion of gaze. Jean-Antoine Houdon perfected this

sculpted gaze in his portrait of Voltaire. Voltaire's eye doesn't look *like* an eye, it *looks* like an eye. Houdon sacrificed one kind of realism for another, opting for a representation of the eye at work.[17]

The German ocularists developed the modern prosthetic glass eye. That glass so serendipitously mimics the tissues of the eye, and that glassblowing is an operation spheric and centric in character seem to me as great a coincidence as the fact that, from the earth, the moon appears the same size as the sun. We keep forgetting that the pupil is a hole, and that the moon is a sphere. In fact, it was Johannes Kepler's pinhole observations of the eclipsed moon that led him to finally understand the relationship between the pupil of the eye and the retina. Kepler was the first to show us that the retina was the crucial interface between light and brain.[18]

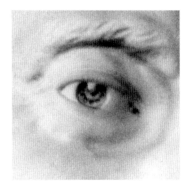

Figure 4b

Just behind the iris of the eye is a second sphincter, the ciliary muscle, which rings the lens and is attached to it by tiny strands called the zonules of Zinn. While the iris is opening or closing its aperture in response to light and dark, the ciliary is contracting or relaxing to accommodate focus. When it is relaxed, the zonules are taut, and the lens is pulled thin to focus on distant things. When it contracts, the zonules go slack, and the lens rebounds into a thicker onion, a shorter focal point, to see things close at hand.[19] ("Lens" comes from the word lentil.) When I hold up my finger in front of my nose and look at it, and then shift my attention to the keyhole beyond it in the door twenty feet away, or when I stoop to look at the keyhole in the gate of #3 Via di Santa Sabina in Rome and then shift to the cupola of St. Peter's it frames two miles away, my eye knows how to make the transfer. How does it know?

I would like to make a series of gel molds of my open eye, so I can study the precise disposition of lids and the folds of tissues around them within the orbit as the eye moves right and left, up and down, even into and out of focus.

A sculptor has a special set of problems in depicting the eye in a self-portrait. I want to get all around the eye: above it, below it, behind it, see what it's doing when it rotates. It is an invasive instinct, for which a mirror, or mirrors, are insufficient. At the instant I look, I change what I'm trying to see. If the eye lights up, what does that look like? Or if it is "looking within"? Or into the future? I need an eye for an eye, an I for an I.

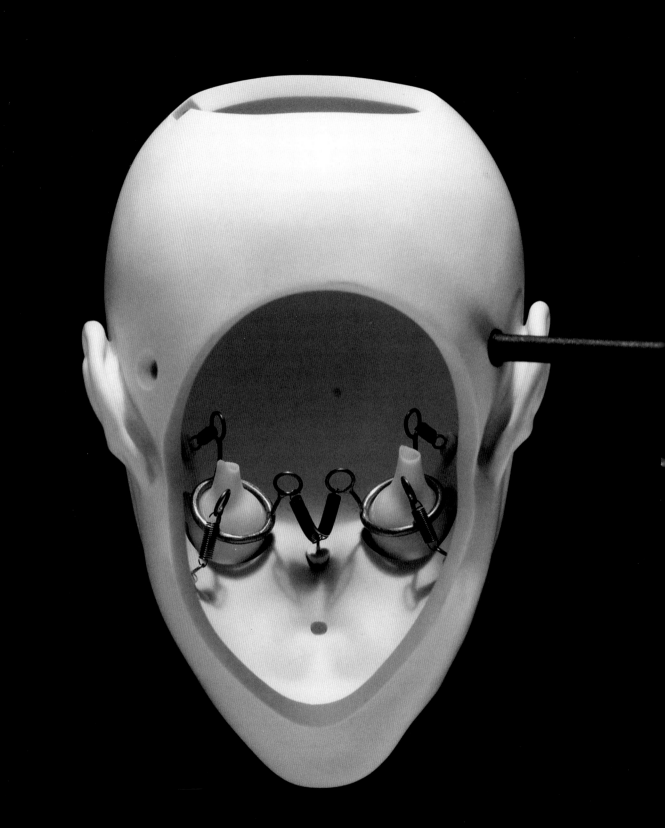

The two biggest problems in fitting the glass eye to the inside of the head are (1) the eye isn't spherical and (2) the porcelain socket, no matter how perfectly I size it, always warps in the kiln.

The eye could be *made* spherical, but that would eliminate the corneal bulge and with it the way light reflects off both the surface of the eye and the surface of the iris. The cornea, living tissue that is transparent, is a tiny magnifying glass placed over the iris's exquisite sphincter. And under this glass the pupil, the name we give to the eye's studious hole, shows us a miniature sun or our own tiny face (the little man) superimposed over the void.

With a clear sense of impending defeat, I proceed to make a set of perfect wooden sizing-balls that I coat with adhesive, then dust with fine carborundum grit, to use as tools for grinding the spherical sockets for each eye inside the head. After each succes-sive firing I get into the head through an opening in the back, and working thus from the inside out, I slowly rotate and rotate a particular-size ball in the negative socket to generate the precise set and diameter for the coming eye, out to the thickness of the eyelid. Sometimes I am lucky and the kiln warp of those thin eyelids coincides with the swell of the cornea.

But then I mount the eyes inside the head with small springs so they are movable, and only one position fits exactly. When the eyes move, little gaps open up between eye and lid. The despair of this! I've got to find a way to make the lids separate from the head, and spring-load those, too, so they can follow the eye. Then the eyes could open and close as well! When things move, exactly how do they move?

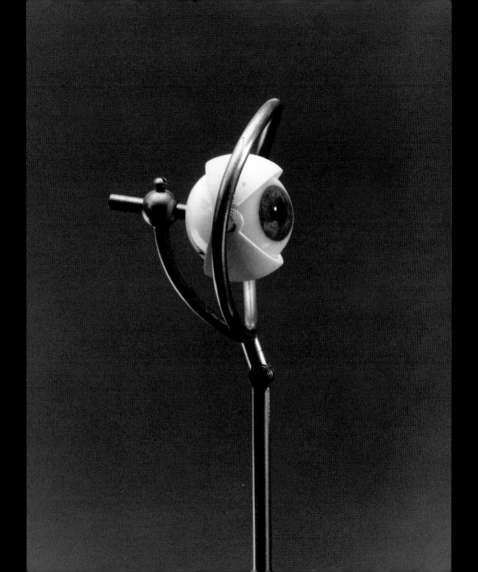

. . . for character and feeling are things we want and need to know about in persons we address, and we are all very skilled in interpreting visual appearance to this end: posture, gesture, glance, the fixed lineaments of the body and the face. In particular we are sensitive to what all these imply of an attitude towards ourselves. . . .

Michael Baxandall is speaking here of the way we transfer this sensitivity to works of art.[20] I sometimes feel that proprioception, our sixth sense, the body's internal knowledge of itself in space, is sculpture's primary realm, one to which vision is only expedient.

I put the figure in different positions and stand back to look at them. A few degrees of shift in the axis of the head to the torso can turn an attentive gesture into an introspective one, or signal a trace of suspicion, or resignation. The most minute changes can induce enormous shifts in our interpretation of gestural intent. The surprise of this, as I move the limbs and the eyes of the figure and register my own involuntary reaction, never fails

me. In literature, one relishes descriptions of the faint, fateful motion at the corner of a character's mouth. The eyes and their lids, in particular, possess a repertoire of tiny movements that seem to have universal readings, such as the imperceptible lifting of the upper lid above the top of the iris, so a little white shows between them.

Even once I've found a specific position for the figure, and adjusted and adjusted for the psychological tension of the pose, the movable joints themselves remain operative in the image and render my decisions unstable. For all my labor, I wonder at this imminent movement and transient arrest.

I notice that in posing the figure I often seek to have it perform eye-hand actions in which the fingers are articulating some difficult task or simulating a close inspection of an imaginary object held up to the light. Or the figure scrutinizes its own hand. It occurs to me that I am having the self-portrait duplicate the same motions I performed in making it.

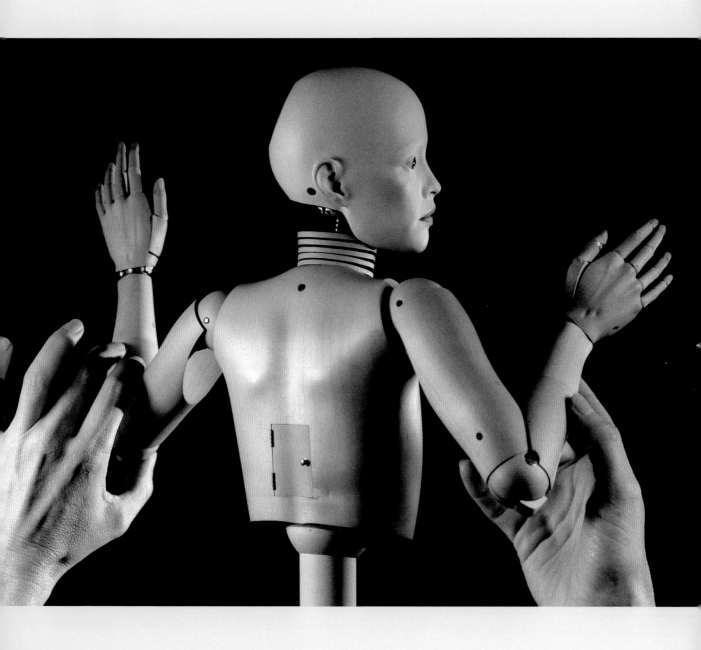

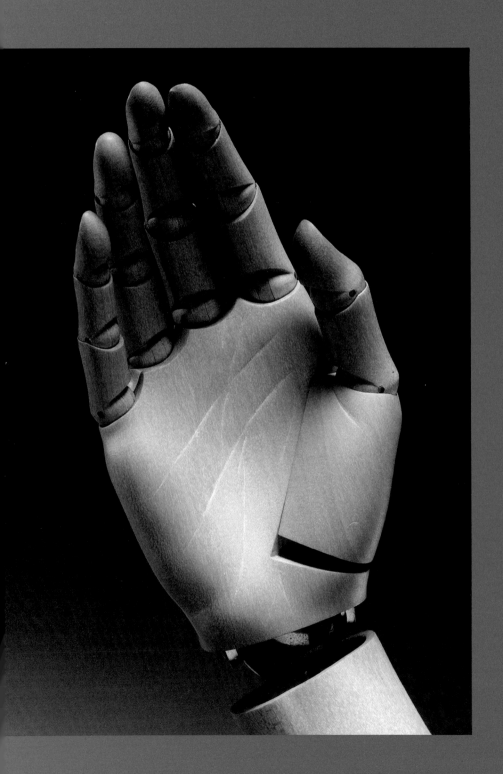

When the "animalcules" (as they were called) in a drop of semen were first viewed under the newly invented microscope, science experienced a moment of astonishment. A number of people thought a tiny homunculus – a complete and perfect microhuman – was constituted in each minute organism. This seventeenth-century discovery came in the context of heated argument over the biological mechanism of conception and embryo formation, and over the relative contributions of male versus female in reproductive generation.[21] Only a few generations before, the alchemist Paracelsus had written his recipe for how to *make* a homunculus. One can see his view of the womb as no more than a nurturing "soil" that could be easily simulated in the laboratory:

Let the semen of a man putrify by itself in a sealed curcurbite (gourd glass) with the highest putrefaction of the venter equinus *(horse dung) for forty days, or until it begins at last to live, move, and be agitated, which can easily be seen. After this time it will be in some degree like a human being, but nevertheless, transparent and without body. If now, after this, it be every day nourished and fed cautiously and prudently with the arcanum of human blood, and kept for forty weeks in the*

perpetual and equal heat of a venter equinus, *it becomes, thenceforth a true and living infant, having all the members of a child that is born from a woman, but much smaller. This we call a homunculus; and it should be afterwards educated with the greatest care and zeal, until it grows and begins to display intelligence. Now, this is one of the greatest secrets which God has revealed to mortal and fallible man.*[22]

A small man made by artifice. If zealously schooled, the alchemist's homunculus-pupil held the promise of becoming a special kind of agent, able to perform tasks beyond the mere powers of ordinary humans. Not unlike Tom Thumb, who was also coming of age about this time, only he was of woman born. And fed a great deal. He is the poet's homunculus.

The notion of growth implicit in all these stories is simple: an already fully formed being, just very tiny, grows a little bigger. Descartes's miniature brain within a brain, the pineal body, shares this feature with early embryology and its notion of a miniature person within a person. But which is the germ cell – sperm or egg?

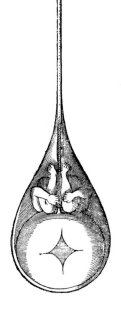

Figure 5

I've been thinking a lot about putrefaction. "High putrefaction." Clay, that biblical substance, is composed of dirt and water and what one might call putrefaction: growing organic matter. The Japanese master potters prepare the clay for the next generation, so it will mold and putrefy for many decades before it is used. This gives it superb plasticity. The Jewish golem is made of clay, and like the homunculus and other living things, it begins small and grows. But the golem continues to grow, and it must be destroyed before it gets too big to control, for it will cease to be a helper and will run amok. *The Polish Jews, after having spoken certain prayers and observed certain fast days, make the figure of a man out of clay or loam which, after they have pronounced the wonder-working* Shem ha-m'phorash *over it, comes to life. It is true this figure cannot speak, but he can to a certain extent understand what one says and*

commands him to do. They call him golem and use him as a servant to do all sorts of housework; he may never go out alone. On his forehead the word Emaeth *(truth: God) is written. But he increases from day to day and can easily become larger and stronger than his house-mates, however small he may have been in the beginning. Being then afraid of him, they rub out the first letter so that nothing remains but* Maeth *(he is dead), whereupon he sinks together and becomes clay again.*[23] "Golem" means unfinished, and is linked to the words for unformed substance in the Bible in Psalm 139, Verse 16, "Thine eyes did see my substance, yet being unperfect."[24] The golem could only be made by a Rabbi, and in addition to the power of the Rabbi's word, some medieval texts required that the maker enter a state of ecstasy before the golem could be brought to life.[25] The very word "ecstasy" means literally "to be beside oneself."[26]

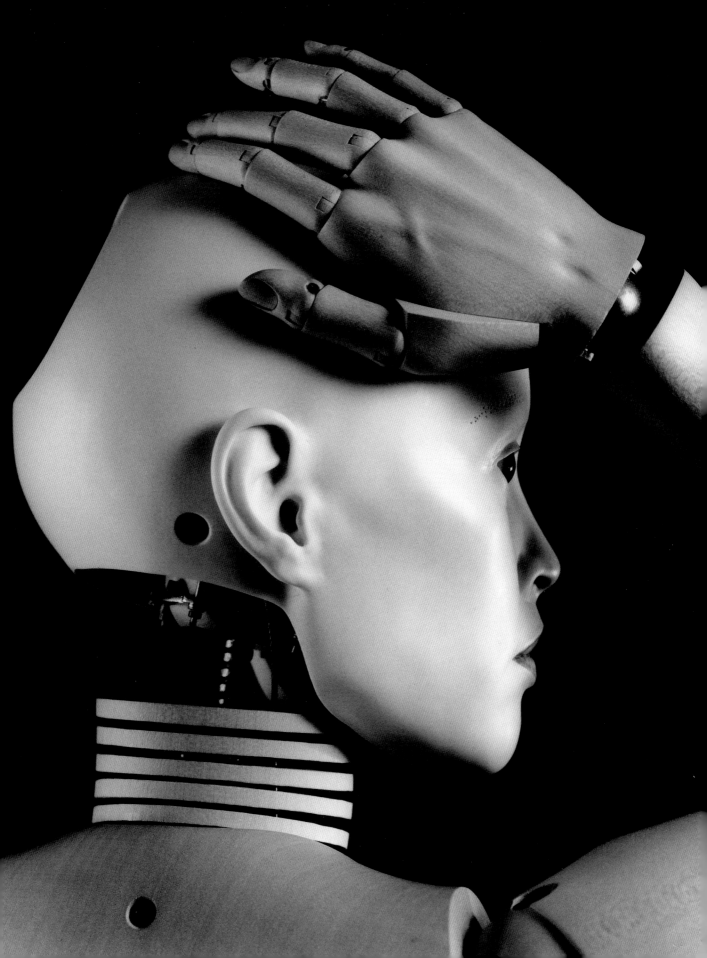

The notion of the illicit copy that suffuses stories of the *doppelgänger* contributes to the sinister tone in E.T.A. Hoffmann's tale "The Sandman" (1815).[27] Two kinds of doubles unnerve us, and one is produced by the other: Coppelius and Coppola, whose joint identity is either discovered or imagined by the character Nathaniel, recognizing the figure that haunted his childhood; and Olympia, the exquisite artificial woman, whose eyes have been made by Coppola, and with whom Nathaniel falls blindly in love. Set at a time when alchemy's shadow extended into a new mechanical age, the clockwork Olympia embodies components of both high technology and black magic.

Olympia, and the double Coppelius/Coppola, are the subject of Freud's essay on the uncanny, a word he defines (after Ernst Jentsch), as describing a state of uncertainty about the extent to which something is or is not alive.[28] By the time Hoffmann wrote his story, a number of famous automata had been constructed by mechanicians of the previous century. And these machines were indeed intended to re-create life. The inventor Baron Wolfgang von Kempelen for example in 1778 completed, after 20 years, a working model of the human vocal organs, inspired by the bagpipe. It had a mouth and flaps resembling the lips and tongue that could form both vowels and consonants.[29] In 1772 Pierre Jaquet-Droz finished his first *écrivain*, a small, seated figure that dipped a quill in an inkstand and wrote anything you liked (*Je ne pense pas... ne serais-Je donc point?* – I do not think ... am I therefore not?), lifting the pen between letters, drawing them with lines of varying thickness, returning to dot an "i," following the pen with its eyes, and pausing from time to time to – think. This little machine could be programmed to write any combination of letters, and contained the entire operating mechanism within its body (drive spring, fusees, gear trains, three sets of forty cams, adjustable alphabet disc, and all the linkages). It is 28 inches tall.[30]

Figure 6

Everyone says the most extraordinary automaton of all time was Vaucanson's duck. Completed in 1738, the duck walked, quacked, ruffled its copper feathers, pecked at grains of food, stretched its neck and actually swallowed the food, and then digested it. In its gut was a miniature chemical laboratory in imitation of the digestive fire, and the natural consequence of this, excretion, the duck also performed.[32] It was nothing less than an attempt to perfectly duplicate a living metabolism. In his journals Goethe describes the duck,[33] which must have fascinated him in relation to the homunculus in *Faust*. And Voltaire wrote with praise for Vaucanson's plans for a human figure that would imitate all the organic functions of the alive body.[34] Instead, Jacques de Vaucanson helped to launch the Industrial Revolution, and the birth of the computer, by designing the prototype for what would later become the Jacquard mechanical loom.

Or take the story of the automaton now in the Franklin Institute in Philadelphia. All but destroyed by fire, the ruined parts of an unidentified machine were given to the Institute in 1928, literally dumped from a truck. An Institute machinist, Charles Roberts, became curious and began to tinker with the brass parts, and in growing earnest started to reassemble them. A miniature boy emerged, seated before a small desk, mounted upon a great console of hidden cams and levers. After years of work, the moment at last came when the parts were reassembled and it became possible to wind the powerful drive springs. With Institute staff watching, the automaton proceeded to introduce itself. Four elaborate drawings, one of a three-masted frigate in full rig; two poems in French, and another in English; and finally in a flourish of penmanship, *Ecrit par L'Automate de Maillardet*.[31]

This was the famous automaton made by Henri Maillardet in London in 1805 and lost in 1833. It had remembered.

Figure 7

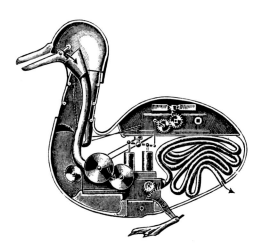

Figure 8

bargain by having Turriano construct a miniature penitent homunculus. A look at this figure in the museum suggests that persons witnessing it in motion in 1560 might actually have believed it to be alive. The uninterrupted repetitive gestures, to us the hallmark of a robot, correspond exactly in this case to the movements of trance.

Can I compare digestion with worship? To attempt to simulate either is entirely fantastic, but with digestion at least there's a way to tell whether you have succeeded or failed. To simulate prayer is a philosophical paradox.

In my mind, an even more uncanny object than the duck is a sixteenth-century automaton of a monk, in the collection of the Smithsonian Institution. The monk is 15 inches tall, made of wood and iron. Driven by a key-wound spring, he walks in a square (the cloister), striking his chest with his right arm, raising and lowering the rosary in his left hand, turning and nodding his head, rolling his eyes, and mouthing silent obsequies. From time to time, he brings the rosary to his lips and kisses it. After over 400 years, he remains in good working order. Tradition attributes his manufacture to one Juanelo Turriano, mechanician to Emperor Charles V. The story goes that the Emperor's son King Philip II, praying at the bedside of his own son who was dying, promised a miracle for a miracle, if his child be spared. When the child did indeed recover, being perhaps none other than Don Carlos himself,[35] the King kept his part of the

Figure 9

English psychologist John Cohen declared in 1966 that there are three things a robot will never be able to do: laugh, blush, or commit suicide.[36] Looking back over the history of automata, it seems that we tried to accomplish the most difficult imitations first, then got more and more humble. Prayer, then eating, then writing... the more complex the machines got, the simpler the functions they performed. Now we have stupendously complicated machines trying to tie their shoe. Certainly we have long since stopped trying to make an artificial memory that *looks* like a little human being.

Perhaps the most interesting development in the history of mechanical memory was Charles Babbage's Analytical Engine, conceived in 1834, and perfected in design over the course of his lifetime (he died in 1871). It was never built, but no one who has since studied Babbage's hundreds of engineering drawings doubts that it would have worked flawlessly. This was a machine capable of calculating mathematical functions to 100 digit results, one that could store and retrieve numbers, conduct numerous operations simultaneously (providing a prototype for distributed processing[37]), use logic to combine them, and correct its own errors. All this was to be accomplished with massive systems of brass and iron toothed gears and drums, in a preelectronic age. "Babbage had a vision of numbers swirling in and out of the mill under control of a *program* contained in punched cards — an idea inspired by the Jacquard loom," Douglas Hofstadter tells us. "Mankind was flirting with mechanized intelligence — particularly if the Engine were capable of 'eating its own tail' (the way Babbage described the Strange Loop created when a machine reaches in and alters its own stored program)."[38] Loops, chains of loops, even nests of them recur in the functional maze of the Analytic Engine.[39] But there was a price. Size. An earlier machine, Babbage's Difference Engine No. 2, recently and laboriously reconstructed at the Science Museum in London, weighs three tons.[40]

Precision, the elimination of human error, was Babbage's great passion, his fundamental impulse, his pathology.

My education in mechanics

For her birthday I would give my mother certificates I designed with colored pencils for 50

free wheelchair cleanings. That was my special job. I still owe her! A really thorough cleaning

took two hours, I polished every spoke and hinge, and developed an assortment of tools

for things like lifting dirt out of the grooves in the foot pedals or untwirling strands of hair

wound around the axles. I admired alike the machine and its occupant and once thought

they were all one thing. She had contracted polio when we were children. While we grew up,

she grew small. Before I was twelve I could carry her.

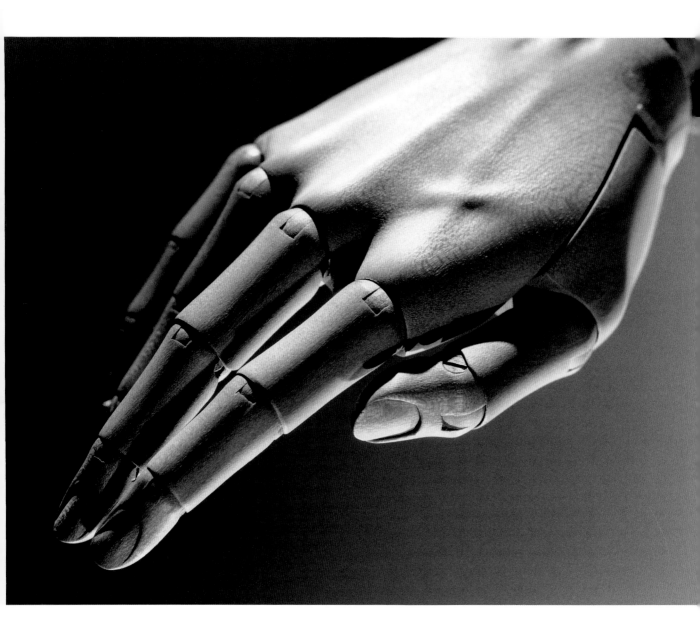

"But what I'd really like to do is get rid of these strings and make the

puppet stand up by itself," I heard myself explain to a friend one day

who was looking at my latest marionette. But what was I saying?! I

dream of a small whole being, able to move around without me. Once

a figure takes on something like a life of its own, I find myself talking

to it, apologizing for removing an arm to repair the elbow. Damage

and repair: these are the two processes I know best, that unfold one

after the other in the studio.

I am propelled by fright and amazement at the coexistence of substance and spirit.

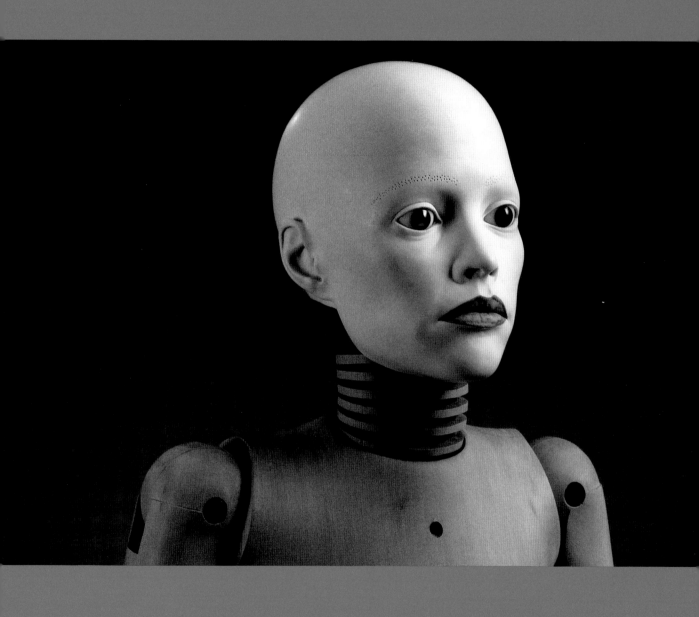

You are gazing at someone asleep, and suddenly become aware that one eye, just slit, has been watching you back.

In microtime: shock. A burst of adrenaline. Attention carries something with it. You feel it even when your back is turned.

Bridge

One may dream, not in plots, but in sensations. The sensation of not being able to push or pull something heavy. The sensation of free fall, of inclination, of pressure. The sensation of being unable to take a deep breath. Many sensations of being inside of something, perhaps something moving out of control, like an elevator that does not stop at the basement but continues to descend. Psychological states are inextricably wound up with these physical sensations, and vice versa.... Then perhaps whole narratives swiftly assemble themselves in the waking.

We always talk about dream or memory as something located in the head. Why do we locate the mind in the head? Brain cells extend the length of the spine – sensory neurons and motor neurons – and from there send out their axons to all perimeters. Remembering is something that goes on all over the body.

This problem of location: we are fascinated with finding the spot where one thing turns into another. The nephew's question of locating the zone where sensation becomes perception, or of locating the "seat" of vision... the question of locating the center of being, of self... the question of where mind ends and body begins... the question of where self ends and world begins: the snake eats its tail.

Such is the poverty of the notion of intent, that it is thought a discrete thing. While we are arguing about the artist's intent or even about self-expression, evolutionary biologists are busy stealing the word "express." Now it refers to the way a feature of an environment, say a visiting bacteria, pulls forth a response in an individual, say a new antibody. The initial action moves backward from circumstance to organism, from outside to in. It isn't even that there is something waiting there to be called forth. The response itself is partly made from the stuff of the irritant. So it's unpredictable. In art's old phrase "self-expression," suddenly the notion of self becomes fluid. What selects and what is selected?

In the darkroom, I continually lose track of the second hand on the clock and leave photos in the stop bath or fixer too long. I'm considering the little "s" sound my mother used to make while talking and working in the kitchen. I practice it. Almost imperceptible, a sort of punctuation, breath held and just released a notch: "s." A kind of miniature exertion. When did I first become aware of it? Was it an awareness accompanied by the realization that I had been hearing it for years? Retrospective attention like this is a mystery of the sensorium. And just like that I've forgotten where the second hand started. One day I tried saying out loud the number on the clock: "Seven!" I called out. And it worked. When the hand came round to seven again I snapped right out of mentally constructing a template for cutting a perfect radius on the lathe, and registered the minute. Incredible! If I actually voice the number so I myself hear it, I'll be able to remember it. It was a small epiphany, not to say a private triumph. But in my exultation and subsequent reverie on the implications of this experience for a theory of memory I forgot to take the paper out of the bath.

My friend Myron complains that I constantly interrupt him. I tell him if I don't

I'll forget something crucial. He accuses me of just blurting out whatever comes

into my head. I insist that my mind is working topologically and interruption

THE VIRTUES AND MISFORTUNES
OF INTERRUPTION

isn't a change of subject as he thinks but rather an increasing number of things

being discussed simultaneously. He says that when I interrupt him *he* forgets what

he is saying. It can be an important decision: to interrupt or to politely listen.

In Chris Marker's film *Sans Soleil* (1982),[41] Japanese crowds shuffle past

vitrines full of the treasures of the Vatican, a great exhibition of the

icons of the Catholic empire that has traveled to Tokyo. The camera

seems to be inside the case, looking back out at the faces peering in.

The people move slowly, taking absent little steps that bump them into

one another, leaning in close, expressionless. We are as close as we

can get to seeing what seeing looks like. On the face of it, looking looks

fairly uneventful. We probably look pretty blank ourselves, sitting in

the theater watching the film. The film, inserting itself in the place of the

work of art, is a membrane through which one crowd studies another.

Everybody here (even Marker once) is paying attention to something

perhaps for the first time. Later, our mouth moves, our eyes light up,

our brows knot. The muscles of the face register recognition. But the

first time we see, we are blind to it.

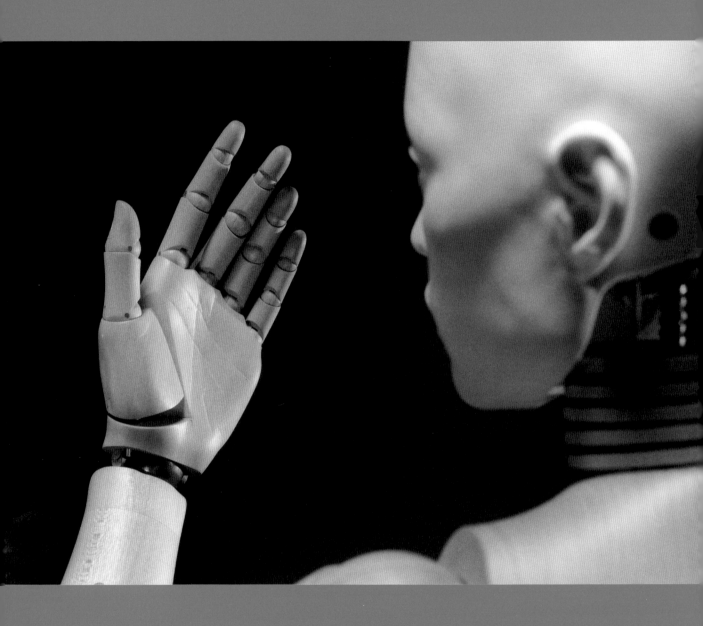

When something transformative happens, you seldom recognize it at the time. An epiphany, a realization of a realization, is a rare occurrence, like a syzygy. Often years go by, and one day you remember you had read – *where* did you read it? – the sentence "We give form to thoughts in order to have them." Who said this, and when did you see it? A vague image of a page hazily forms in the mind, with two columns – a not-very-good xerox – two-thirds of the way down on the left. You tear your entire library apart looking for it, heart pounding when you think you're getting close. Where were you living at the time?...You get out all your files from 1983, appalled at what you thought was worth saving that year. Everything but the thing you now want. No time to weed this out now, might need something later, wasn't it in the spring? Suddenly, hideous doubt sends the blood to your face: could you have actually had it in your hand this morning? You double back and retrace what you just searched in case it was sitting there in plain view all along. Just when you consciously consult your memory, it plays a thousand tricks. No direct route. We must perform for it the exact set of steps and bows, in precise order. And we think we are the master of ourselves.

1 Gaston Bachelard, *The Poetics of Space*, trans. Maria Jolas (Boston: Beacon Press, 1964), 164–66.

2 *The Complete Fairy Tales of the Brothers Grimm*, trans. Jack Zipes (New York: Bantam Books, 1987), 143–44. Translation based in part on the first edition of the *Kinder- und Hausmärchen*, published in two volumes in 1812 and 1818 by Jacob and Wilhelm Grimm.

3 The link between the word "pupil" and the Greek word κόρη, korē, is taken from *The American Heritage Dictionary of the English Language*, 1971. This is also the source for the following etymology of the word "homunculus."

4 David C. Lindberg, *Theories of Vision from Al-Kindi to Kepler* (Chicago: University of Chicago Press, 1976), 93. I must thank Evelyn Lincoln for introducing me to this book, and in it to Lindberg's presentation of Adelard. Lindberg's primary sources for Adelard are German and English translations from the original Latin: *Die Quaestiones naturales des Adelardus von Bath*, in Beiträge zur Geschichte der Philosophie des Mittelalters, ed. Martin Müller, vol. 31, pt. 2, Münster, 1934; and *Questiones naturales*, in Berachya Hanakdan, *Dodi Ve-Nechdi (Uncle and Nephew) ... To Which is Added the First English Translation from the Latin of Adelard of Bath's Quaestiones naturales*, ed. and trans. Hermann Gollancz, Oxford, 1920.

5 Lindberg, *Theories of Vision*, 93–4.

6 Ibid., 94.

7 Daniel Dennett, *Consciousness Explained* (Boston: Little, Brown and Company, 1991), 196.

8 Elliot Eisner, "What Do Children Learn When They Paint?" *Art Education* 31, no. 3 (March 1978): 10. Eisner said, "Some aspects of artistic thinking are inherent in the human condition, such as the need to confer form upon ideas and feelings in order to have them."

9 And κόρη or Kore, the little Greek girl and pupil of the eye, is Persephone, who makes the greatest round-trip of all, year after year, to the underworld and back. (From a conversation with Douglas Chismar, on the Eleusinian mysteries.)

10 David Sylvester, *Looking at Giacometti* (New York: Henry Holt, 1994), from chapter 5, "The Residue of a Vision," 28. The Giacometti quotation in this passage originally comes from "Entretien avec David Sylvester" in *Alberto Giacometti: Écrits*, ed. Michel Leiris and Jacques Dupin (Paris: Hermann, 1990), 288.

11 Stuart Hampshire, "A New Way of Seeing," in *The New York Review of Books* XLII, no. 12 (July 13, 1995): 47. In this review of Sylvester's book, Hampshire includes a translation of the next sentence of Giacometti's comment. See *Écrits*, ed. Leiris and Dupin, 288.

12 Wayne Thiebaud, "A Personal View of Drawing and Painting," Duncan Phillips Lecture, October 20, 1992, The Phillips Collection, Washington, D.C.

13 Donald Keene, *Bunraku: the Art of the Japanese Puppet Theater*, photographs by Kaneko Hiroshi (Tokyo: Kodansha International, 1965), 20.

14 Ibid., 239. Keene gives the following caption: "Gabu: The name is of uncertain

origin. It designates a head which at first appears to be that of a beautiful young girl, but when the operator pulls a string turns into an ogress: the mouth opens to reveal hideous, pointed gold teeth; gold-rimmed eyes pop open; and gold horns emerge from the head. Used for women who are actually demons, like Kiyohime in *Hidakagawa Iriaizakura* (1759), an adaptation of the Nō play *Dōjōji*." Photographs by Keizo Kaneko, formerly Kaneko Hiroshi.

15 Distributed by New American Cinema Group/Film-Makers' Cooperative, New York City.

16 "Painters always want more of the *hereness* of sculpture, and sculptors always want more of the *thereness* of painting," the sculptor Myron Helfgott said one day to his students.

17 I am grateful to the Wildenstein Institute, Paris, for the use of this photograph of Houdon's *Voltaire* taken by H.H. Arnason. The photo appears in Arnason's book *The Sculptures of Houdon* (New York: Oxford University Press, 1975), plate 56. Arnason writes, "Houdon had many different techniques for rendering the eyes. Sometimes he bored a deep hole in the center of the pupil; sometimes, often in children's portraits, he bored a circle of small holes to create a star-like effect for the iris. Most frequently he cut out the entire iris, bored a deeper hole for the pupil and, by allowing a small fragment of the material to overhang the iris, established an illusionistic effect of light and shadow that made the eye actually appear to move" (p. 20).

18 Lindberg, *Theories of Vision*, 178–208.

19 See Jane F. Koretz and George H.

Handelman, "How the Human Eye Focuses," *Scientific American* 259, no. 1 (July 1988): 92–9.

20 Michael Baxandall, *The Limewood Sculptors of Renaissance Germany* (New Haven: Yale University Press, 1980), 153.

21 For the homunculus of the theory of preformation, see Arthur William Meyer, *The Rise of Embryology* (Palo Alto, Cal.: Stanford University Press, 1939), 62–85. See also Clara Pinto-Correia, *The Ovary of Eve: Egg and Sperm and Preformation* (Chicago: University of Chicago Press, 1997), in particular the chapter entitled "The H Word," though I hardly agree that "homunculus," as a word, has so bad a reputation.

22 I first encountered Paracelsus' recipe in John Cohen's wonderful book *Human Robots in Myth and Science* (London: George Allen and Unwin, 1966). His source for the recipe is the English translation of Paracelsus' writings by Arthur Edward Waite: *The Hermetic and Alchemical Writings of Aureolus Philippus Theophrastus Bombast, of Hohenheim, Called Paracelsus The Great* (London: James Elliott, 1894), 124.

23 Robert Plank, "The Golem and the Robot," *Literature and Psychology* XV, no. 1 (Winter 1965): 13. This is Plank's translation of Jacob Grimm's 1808 description of the legend of the golem.

24 Ibid., 14.

25 Cohen, *Human Robots in Myth and Science*, 39–42. Cohen cites Eleazar of Worms, c. 1160–1230, and his Commentary on the *Sefer Yezirah*, for one such recipe for making a golem.

26 When I related this recipe to the late poet Larry Levis, he said "Why, yes! And the word ecstasy means to be outside

of oneself." Later, reading his poem "Elegy with a Petty Thief in the Rigging," (Larry Levis, *Elegy*, Pittsburgh: University of Pittsburgh Press, 1997), I saw why he knew this word so well.

27 E.T. A. Hoffmann, *Tales of Hoffmann*, trans. R. J. Hollingdale (London: Penguin, 1982).

28 Sigmund Freud, "The 'Uncanny,'" 1919, in *On Creativity and the Unconscious*, selected and annotated by Benjamin Nelson (New York: Harper and Row, 1958), 122–61, especially page 132.

29 Cohen, *Human Robots in Myth and Science*, 84–5.

30 See Alfred Chapuis and Edmond Droz, *Automata: A Historical and Technological Study*, trans. Alec Reid (Neuchâtel: Editions du Griffon, 1958), 292–5; and Roland Carrera and David Fryer, "Androids," *FMR*, no. 6 (November 1984): 65–92.

31 Charles F. Penniman, Jr., "Maillardet's Automaton," The Franklin Institute Science Museum, Philadelphia, unpublished manuscript, 1975; and article, "Philadelphia's 179 Year Old Android," *BYTE Publications*, vol. 3, no. 8 (August 1978): 90–4. Mr. Penniman has long been associated with the Maillardet automaton, including its recent restoration, maintenance, and demonstration. He has also made an extensive study of its mechanism and history.

32 Chapuis, *Automata*, 233–42.

33 Ibid., 234.

34 Jean-Claude Beaune, "The Classical Age of Automata: An Impressionistic Survey from the Sixteenth to the Nineteenth Century," in *Fragments for a History of the Human Body, Part One*, ed. Michel Feher (Cambridge, Mass.: MIT Press/Zone, 1989), 457.

35 The connection between the mechanical monk and Don Carlos has yet to be conclusively demonstrated. Three facts compel the link. One is Turriano's reputation for comparable mechanical feats. The second is the probable date of manufacture of the little machine. The third is the well-documented illness of Don Carlos in 1562. After the best physicians of the Spanish court (including Andreas Vesalius himself), failed to bring about a cure, a miraculous recovery was effected when a desperate procession of townspeople removed the preserved mummy of a Franciscan holy man, Fray Diego de Alcalá, from the Church of Saint Francis, and carried it to the royal bedroom where they placed it in the patient's bed with him. This miracle led to the canonization of San Diego by Pope Sixtus V. For a superb description of Don Carlos's illness, see L. J. Andrew Villalon, "Putting Don Carlos Together Again: Treatment of a Head Injury in Sixteenth-Century Spain," *Sixteenth Century Journal* XXVI, no. 2 (1995): 347–65. I myself have tried to put together all extant information on the automaton in my forthcoming article "Clockwork Prayer: A Sixteenth Century Mechanical Monk."

36 Cohen, *Human Robots in Myth and Science*, 137. I first encountered this passage as quoted in full in Beaune's article, "The Classical Age of Automata," in *Fragments for a History of the Human Body*, ed. Michel Feher, 469–71 (see note 34).

37 Anthony Hyman, *Charles Babbage: Pioneer of the Computer* (Oxford: Oxford University Press, 1982), 242.

38 Beaune, "The Classical Age of Automata," 460–61, quoting from Douglas R.

Hofstadter, *Gödel, Escher, Bach: an Eternal Golden Braid* (New York: Basic Books, 1979), 25. I owe my dawning understanding of the connections between Vaucanson, Jacquard, and Babbage to Beaune's article.

39 *Babbage's Calculating Engines: A Collection of Papers by Henry Prevost Babbage,* with an introduction by Allan G. Bromley, The Charles Babbage Institute Reprint Series for the History of Computing (Los Angeles: Tomash, 1982), p. xvi, from the original edition published by Spon & Co., London, 1889. And I owe thanks to mathematician James Deveney for contributing to my understanding of Babbage's accomplishment.

40 Doron D. Swade, "Redeeming Charles Babbage's Mechanical Computer," *Scientific American* 268, no. 2 (February 1993): 86–91.

41 Distributed by Argos Films.

Credits

Unless otherwise noted, all photographs are by Katherine Wetzel.

Pages 11, 14, 17, 20, 23, 25, 26, 31, 37, 41, 42, 45, 46, 51, 52, 55, 56, 61, 64, 67, 71, 72, 75, 77, and 78: Elizabeth King, *Pupil*, 1987–90. Porcelain, glass eyes, carved wood (Swiss pear), brass. Dimensions variable. Figure is one-half life-size. Collection the Hirshhorn Museum and Sculpture Garden, Washington, D.C.

Pages 13, 19, 32, 35, 39, and 69: Elizabeth King, work in progress, 1996–present. Porcelain, glass eyes, carved wood, metals, eyelashes, fiber optics. Head is 5 x 3¾ x 4½ inches.

Page 28: a view of the studio, 1995.

Pages 4, 33: Elizabeth King, *Plans for Movable Neck and Shoulder Joints* (detail and full plan), 1988. Cut paper, 24½ x 36½ x 2 inches. Collection the artist.

Page 6: Elizabeth King, *Plans for Movable Hands* (detail), 1991. Cut paper, 17 x 21 x 2 inches. Collection Kenneth L. Freed, Boston, Mass.

Page 49: Elizabeth King, *Idea for a Mechanical Eye*, 1988–90. Cast acrylic, brass, wood. Eyeball diameter ⅞ inch; eye, eyelids and socket each move independently. Collection the artist.

Figures

Figure 1: Illustration by Eleanor Quarrie, after George Cruikshank, for the binding label of *Grimm's Folk Tales*, 1949. © The Folio Society, Ltd., London.

Figure 2: Illustration by Paul Weiner, from *Consciousness Explained*, by Daniel Dennett, 1991. Copyright © 1991 by Daniel Dennett. By permission of Little, Brown and Company.

Figures 3a, 3b: "Gabu" photographs by Keizo Kaneko, formerly Kaneko Hiroshi, as seen in the book *Bunraku, The Art of the Japanese Puppet Theater*, by Donald Keene, Kodansha International Ltd., 1965. My grateful thanks to Mr. Kaneko for allowing the reproduction of his work.

Figures 4a, 4b: From *The Sculptures of Houdon*, by H. H. Arnason, Oxford University Press, 1975. Photograph by the author, courtesy the Wildenstein Institute, Paris. *Voltaire*, by Jean-Antoine Houdon, 1781, marble, collection the State Hermitage Museum, Inc., Leningrad.

Figure 5: Woodcut by Nicolaus Hartsoeker (1656–1725), from his *Éssai de dioptrique* (Paris: J. Anisson, 1694), 230. A human spermatozoon containing a homunculus. Courtesy The Wellcome Institute Library, London.

Figure 6: The Jaquet-Droz writing automaton, 1772, in the Neuchâtel Museum of Art and History; photograph from Alfred Chapuis and Edmond Droz, *Automata: A Historical and Technological Study,* trans. Alec Reid, 1958. First published in French in 1949. By permission of Editions du Griffon, Neuchâtel (Switzerland).

Figure 7: A drawing made recently by Henri Maillardet's automaton of 1805. Courtesy The Historical and Interpretive Collections of The Franklin Institute, Philadelphia, Pa.

Figure 8: Diagram of Jacques de Vaucanson's mechanical duck of 1738. Engraving, nineteenth century. Photograph: Deutsches Museum, Munich.

Figure 9: Automaton figure of a monk, South Germany or Spain, c. 1560. Attributed to Juanelo Turriano. Photograph courtesy the National Museum of American History, Smithsonian Institution, Washington, D.C.

Acknowledgments

The challenge to make this book came from three friends at the Mary Ingraham Bunting Institute at Radcliffe College where we were Fellows in 1996–97: Farah Jasmine Griffin, Fran Peavey, and A. J. Verdelle. A. J. set the stakes.

I thank and honor Florence Ladd, then Director of the Bunting Institute; and I thank Lindy Hess, Director of the Radcliffe Publishing Course, whom I met through Florence; and Doe Coover, my agent, whom I met through Lindy. Renny Harrigan, Lyn O'Conor, and Gretchen Elmendorf, at the Bunting, were extraordinary.

The Hirshhorn Museum and Sculpture Garden in Washington, D.C. owns the piece *Pupil*, and I am grateful to James Demetrion, Phyllis Rosenzweig, and Brian Kavanagh who arranged several loans of the sculpture, making possible the long collaborative sessions with Katherine Wetzel.

The photographer Eric Beggs, whose beloved late sister Barbara Bini photographed my work so many years ago in Rome – only by chance did I discover they were brother and sister – helped me begin to think about how this book could look. We worked together following an exhibition at the Huntington Gallery, University of Texas at Austin, where the sculpture was on view. I tried poses, he took test pictures. Even though I pose the figure for each exhibition, and the gesture is crucial to the work as seen, this was the first time I pushed to discover what this piece could really do. The opportunity to begin this work was made possible at the Huntington by Curator Annette Carlozzi and Registrar Sue Ellen Jeffers.

I thank three superb research assistants: Harvard students Syau-Jyun Liang and Bulbul Tiwari, and Virginia Commonwealth University student Adam Meuse. Charles Bleick, Acting Director of the VCU Anderson Gallery in 1997, administered the borrowing of the sculpture from the Hirshhorn and created the time and space for Katherine and myself to set up our "laboratory." As ever, without my colleagues in the Sculpture Department at VCU, and the uncommon quality and exuberance they give my life in academia, I would be at a loss. I thank the VCU School of the Arts for granting me research leave to accept the Bunting Fellowship.

Michael More at Eastman Kodak Company provided the film for the project. Kirk Schroder saved the whole show at least once.

I have shamelessly pursued Celeste Goodridge, Myron Helfgott, Jane Kamensky, Maya Carlson, Ashley Kistler, Richard Carlyon, and Katharine Lee for their advice.

Claudia Stone and Allan Stone, of the Allan Stone Gallery in New York, supported this project in countless ways, as they have supported me in as many ways, for a very long time.

To Paul Gottlieb, I owe the greatest thanks of all, for the pure opportunity to do this, to take an idea and make an actual thing out of it, an object with properties and being. And to Kathy Doyle: what good fortune to work with you at Abrams. Judith Hudson's design for this book astonishes me.

My deepest gratitude is for Gail Mazur; for Evelyn Lincoln; for Katherine Wetzel, who captures the life of the sculpture on film; and for Carlton Newton, who asks, "and what is behind the nen?"

87

EDITOR: Katherine Rangoon Doyle
DESIGNER: Judith Hudson

Quotations from the Epigraph page come
from the following sources:

Katsuki Sekida, *Zen Training: Methods and Philosophy,* ed. A.V. Grimstone (Tokyo: Weatherhill,
1983), 110

Jacob Bronowski, *The Origins of Knowledge
and Imagination* (New Haven: Yale University
Press, 1978), 94–95. Copyright © 1978 by
Yale University

LIBRARY OF CONGRESS
CATALOGING-IN-PUBLICATION DATA

King, Elizabeth, 1950–
Attention's loop: a sculptor's reverie on the
coexistence of substance and spirit / Elizabeth
King; photographs by Katherine Wetzel.
    p.   cm.
ISBN 0–8109–1998–2 (hardcover)
1. King, Elizabeth, 1950– —Psychology.
2. Mind and body. 1. Title.
NB237.K49A2 1999
730'.92—dc21   98–40319

Printed and bound in Japan

Harry N. Abrams, Inc.
100 Fifth Avenue
New York, N.Y. 10011
www.abramsbooks.com